Dedicated to my family.
I love you all.

NO RESERVE

A MEMOIR

CHAPTER ONE

LOAD "$", 8

Not too far outside the city limits of Detroit still lie endless rows of Cape Cod homes, each more unassuming than the next. Dearborn was one of those older suburbs, methodically filling in the fringes of the city in the 1930s.

As I drove closer to my destination, I imagined this modest street in its day as a Technicolor-perfect snapshot of Americana. On this cold, gray morning it was ever more apparent its light had gone out long ago, leaving just another sorry rust belt casualty.

LOT #1 DEARBORN, MICHIGAN

My three hour road trip from my home in Goshen, Indiana was finally closing in on its end.

My lower back was starting to ache and standing up and walking around for a few minutes was just what I needed. I carefully watched my GPS zero in on my stop.

.4 miles ...

.1 miles ...

Then my destination would be on the right.

"This must be it," I thought. I parked in the street and marched over the buckled sidewalk to the front door of the house. Three knocks summoned a short greasy-haired man, his wife and their cat.

I was invited inside. It was a small bungalow with the typical one-car garage tucked way in the back. The house smelled of urine and cigarettes. On a desk sat two Commodore 64 computers, two disk drives, a monitor and some floppy disk games.

This is what I was here for.

Cloaked over everything was easily three decades of accumulated dust. I was certain these computers hadn't moved an inch since 1984. I wasn't shocked at all. It fit the house; it fit the owners.

I walked over to inspect the hardware. The floor canted a bit towards the front porch. The seller was quick to assure me everything worked the last time he

used them. "Yeah, but how long ago was that?"
I thought. Probably around the last time this guy took
a bath.

I could have had him hook the computers up on
the spot to verify they worked, but I decided to take
his word for it as the smell of the house was quickly
burning my nostrils. I handed the man his cash,
petted their cat, and loaded up the haul. After a
couple massive sneezing fits, I started on my journey
back home.

It it was December, 2015 and if you dared to blink
your eye, you'd miss the sun's elusive appearance for
another month. I really did despise this time of the
year. It was the short days more than the cold that did
me in. I needed the daylight; I needed projects to keep
me active. It was cold, dark and I had nothing to
do outside.

I had been browsing some Craigslist ads a few
days prior to my trip. The plan I hatched was to go
out and find an old Commodore 64 computer just
like the one I had as a kid. My intention was to play a
game I loved from my childhood. And that is what led
me to Dearborn. I'd play a few games, have a little
nostalgic fun and kill some time until I saw the sun
once again.

Once home, I brought my haul down to the basement. I set up a makeshift desk, borrowing my oldest son's Lego table I had built for him. It was time to set up my computers and test them out. I unraveled the mega-sized cat toy of wires I acquired. Luckily, I had all the cords I needed. The first computer was hooked up and switched on.

No blips, no static–nothing but a blank screen.

"Crap!"

"Did I just get duped?" I thought.

Did I just drive all that way for nothing? I had an immediate sinking feeling that was just taken by this guy and I had nothing more than a pile of old junk.

I still had another computer to try out. There was still a chance this was not all just a big bust. I carefully reconnected the power cord to the second computer. I took my time, making sure everything was securely connected. I took a deep breath and flipped on the power switch.

A full second passed ...

and then ...

Boom!

9

The old startup prompt came back to life:

```
**** COMMODORE 64 BASIC V2 ****
64K RAM SYSTEM 38911 BASIC BYTES FREE
READY
```

There it was. Sweet victory! The welcome screen I knew so well was alive once again.

The Commodore 64 debuted in the early 1980s. It came along just as the Atari 2600 was fading in popularity. When it was first launched, there was no desktop with cute little icons for the user to click on; there wasn't even a mouse. What the user had to do was give it a command in the basic computer language it understood by using the keyboard.

The Commodore 64 was a very popular computer at the time; it sold millions of units. It was marketed as a home computer. The user could run word processing and spreadsheet software if they wanted to, and many people did. But many more simply played games on it.

Telengard was the one and only game I saved from my childhood. *Telengard* was a fantasy role playing game. The point of the game was simple. The player controlled a character that was sent to a dark dungeon on a quest to battle all kinds of fierce monsters and acquire riches.

Your character would explore a vast maze, picking up treasures along the way as well as other objects like swords and potions. If your character had enough experience, it was awarded the next level. That came with additional hit points, more advanced spells and the chance to slay even tougher monsters. It was instantly addicting for my 12-year-old self.

How much treasure could I collect? What level could I achieve? I logged many hours on that game, and I was very good at it. I still remembered the computer's primary command like it was yesterday:

```
LOAD"$",8
```

That command would tell the computer to read the contents of the floppy disk. Then the user simply typed in the name of the program they wanted.

I played a few games of *Telengard*. I wasn't rusty at all; everything came right back to me. It was fun for a couple of hours. I got to level 12 before being killed by a fire-breathing dragon, the toughest monster in the game. I showed my two young boys just to get their reactions. To them, this was a blocky relic from the past and it received a collective "meh."

My itch was scratched, but I didn't feel any more content that winter. I went back to my normal routine, riding out my seasonal affective disorder. The computers sat dormant in the basement storage area for the next couple of months.

CHAPTER TWO

THE OBSESSION BEGINS

Springtime arrived and with it much needed sunlight and warmth. I had a renewed energy in me. It was time to tackle some outdoor projects and also clear out those computers. The place to do it was ebay.

I had sold some things on ebay from time to time since I became a member in 1998. I auctioned off all sorts of random items I was either tired of or had replaced. I like to keep one small box full old keepsakes—just for nostalgia's sake—no more, no less. Anything more than that got weeded out and liquidated. I was familiar with the ebay selling process and I had a 100% positive feedback rating racked up. I knew this was the place to get rid of the goods.

My listings were the cut and dry variety, straight to the point. I didn't need to oversell. I had a perfect rating. All my computers and disk drives acquired in Dearborn sold very quickly, and I soon learned what I could make on each particular item.

This was not the beginning of my obsession. Though I had just doubled my money. I didn't think too much of it, I figured I just got lucky. Flipping these full time for a profit had not even crossed my mind.

LOT #2 LA GRANGE, INDIANA

I found myself bored one day and back on Craigslist searching for more Commodore computers. An ad was recently posted with a seller that claimed to have an entire attic full of old computers and games. Maybe lightening could strike twice, I thought. Maybe I could make another nice profit. I made arrangements to check out the lot.

La Grange, Indiana is another world away from Dearborn. It's a small speck on the map just east of Shipshewana, Indiana. The route there was U.S. 20, a major east-west artery just south of the Indiana toll road that carried a steady flow of semi trucks and horse-drawn buggies. This was of course the heart of RV and Amish county.

I headed out on a warm Saturday morning. Springtime was in full swing and I was in a completely different frame of mind. I had so much I could do now. No longer confined to the indoors, my winter slump was over. The day was actually quite summerlike–the outside temperature gauge in my SUV read 70 degrees.

GPS once again guided me to my destination. To my surprise, the house actually was an old school. It was an early 1900s brick building with a two-story gabled entryway and a classroom on each side. Strewn across the front of the property were at least five old vehicles, among them a Volkswagen Beetle, a black 1940s Ford and an RV.

After a couple knocks at the open back door, a man in his 50s in shorts and a dirty white T-shirt waddled up to greet me. I introduced myself and walked inside.

I was immediately taken aback by the building. I thought it had the potential to be a really awesome house, with a lot of work–well, that and calling the TV show *Hoarders* first. The building had a wide, corridor running down the middle of it. It was very dark, I could not even see to the front from where I was standing. There most likely was a pile of junk blocking the view anyways. One room in the back appeared to be an old office. Still inside was a large desk and an old phone mounted to the wall. Piled on top of the desk were boxes, random papers and old mail.

The seller explained that he had a computer store in the 1980s and just kept the inventory after the it closed. He was getting ready to move and needed to clear out some space. Maybe that is why he had such a low asking price. There was a Commodore 64 computer, multiple disk drives, monitors and many games. He explained what everything was one by one, giving me the back story of almost every item. I knew what they were already, but I pretended to listen anyways.

The seller had an even bigger lot of equipment than the man in Dearborn. He said he wanted to basically shock me with sheer the amount of stuff he had. Oh, he had plenty of junk alright, but this junk was now slowly becoming my treasure.

I loaded up the SUV as quickly as I could. As I was trying to make my escape, the man walked over to me. He leaned over and rested his arms on the windowsill of the car and stood face to face with me. He was well into my personal space at this point.

The SUV was running, but I couldn't back up.
I had strange feeling he was about to lay something big on me.

He proceeded to tell me story about a man that got busted for hacking NASA with his Commodore 64 back in the 1980s. The man was forced to expunge everything computer-related he owned to avoid persecution. With a smug smile and a twinkle in his eye he waited for my response.

"No way bro! You?" I replied as I quickly played along with his delusional story.

"Get me the heck out of here!" I thought. I suppose the Pentagon was next on his list. Maybe the White House! I must have missed that headline that read,

"THE U.S. NOW STANDS
AT DEFCON 4."

I continued to play captivated until I could break free. He ate it up.

A scene straight from *The Dukes of Hazzard* played out as I screeched out of the property. Soon I was back dodging horse manure on my way home. I was feeling very excited at the sheer amount of vintage goodness I just scored, especially at the steal I got it for.

I immediately sorted through everything. This time around, there was a lot more software. There were some old titles I recognized, but at this point I was done playing games.

The real fun was not just in reselling old computer hardware, that was fairly mundane. What made it more like a treasure hunt for me was uncovering the software–those old floppy disk games that had to "load" for a couple minutes to be ready.

Most games were the run of the mill variety, with thousands still in circulation, but if you were lucky, you came across some rarities. Those would return big bucks. That is what the ebay nerds were after. They wanted these games. "Oh, I'd give them games," I thought, rolling my hands like a mad scientist. I'd give them all the games they can handle!

The second lot was immediately pieced out and resold. No playing games, no reminiscing, just right down to business. My items sold quickly, and I did very well with this haul, much better than the first lot. It was at this point just like a crack addict, I was officially hooked.

CHAPTER THREE

THE HOME OFFICE

My new computer flipping office turned out to be my basement. It served as a warehouse to store all the new inventory, as well as the assembly line for processing everything. Once a new load was acquired, I would bring everything downstairs as one giant pile. I didn't like to start on my tasks until all the items were down there at once–then the weeding out could begin.

Items of no value, usually printers, were tossed save for a few in brand new condition; they could be resold. Anything else that couldn't make much money: business software, floppy disks with personal information or anything that was broken, was whipped across the room like a Frisbee into the trash.

We finished our basement three years after my wife Marci and I built our house. One half of the space contained floor to ceiling built-in cabinets with the main computer hub of the home on one side of the room and the TV area for the kids on the other.

On the other half of the basement was the game room, complete with darts, a pinball machine and wet bar. The centerpiece was the billiards table. A 1912 Brunswick Richelieu. A mahogany beauty with thick, solid legs. The kind you rarely see these days. It had a few surface flaws, but the bones were there. It was a hand-me-down from my dad who acquired it in the mid 1980s as his basement crown jewel. I spent hours playing on that pool table as a kid.

My dad taught me all the basics, how to rack the pool balls, the correct pool cue grip, even the impressive back spin technique. It was left in my parents house when they sold it in 1995 for the new owners to use. The new owners enjoyed it as their own until it was eventually picked up. In 2011, the pool table made its way to me.

The pool table movers even marveled at it; they took pictures and noted how you rarely see old models like this anymore. I was beaming with excitement the day I finally received it.

The felt had been changed to a lovely baby poop yellow sometime in the 1990s. It had many marks and a couple tears on it. A full reconditioning was in order. I had the railing sanded down and re-stained. Marci and I chose a nice classic dark green color for the new felt. After the overhaul, it looked brand new again.

That Christmas, Marci surprised me with a heavy-duty vinyl cover for it. She was very proud of herself, having measured the table on her own for a perfect fit. We enjoyed the pool table at a few parties and some games with neighbors. But that time was short-lived.

I needed a work area for my new found computer picking obsession and the pool table turned out to be it. The cover went on.

It would remain covered for the next three years.

CHAPTER FOUR

MEET ME IN ST. LOUIS

My wife Marci and I have been married for thirteen years. She is the most thoughtful person I have ever known. She loves to do for others, always willing to offer encouragement. Marci has a gift for making people feel special. It is something that comes very naturally for her. She is also a first born like myself.

We are both very driven to be successful. Sometimes I think we both may be a little too goal oriented. I know we make an unstoppable team when it comes to setting up the Christmas decorations. We are like a well-oiled machine.

I retrieve all ten bins from the attic; she sets up the nativity set and tree. The whole process is knocked out on the Friday after Thanksgiving. It has been every year without fail since 2005.

Marci and I had been toying with the idea of putting in swimming pool–this came on the heels of a couple of raises for both of us. At first, just uttering the word had both of us looking at each other with a "you can't be serious" look. This was something we never even considered. But once the idea was planted, it stayed there and would not go away. After many weeks of consideration, we agreed that this swimming pool would be something we wanted to do for our children. We made a plan.

We were going to go for it.

LOT #8 ST. LOUIS, MISSOURI

I found lot #8 a mere 400 miles away. A new Craigslist ad was posted at just the right time as my inventory was waning. I normally kept my searches a little closer to home, but one city search led to the next neighboring city, which led to the next. Before I knew it, I had a doozy of a trip ahead of me. I had to travel the western half of Indiana and all of Illinois, from top to bottom, all in a day.

Marci is very supportive in everything I do. She always makes sure to compliment me on my hard work. But she also has her perspective on my new "job."

"That is so far for you to go," she said.

Of course I can make the drive, I thought. I'm a grown man. I didn't see any need for concern.

"Don't worry, I got this," I assured her.

She could handle the kids on her own that day. I was going to make some good money. It was an even trade off in my mind; I had convinced myself of that from the beginning.

What I liked to do when I had a load to pick up the next day is to get up bright and early and hit the road before sunrise. That was primarily to get back as soon as I could and not disrupt the schedule at home. There was another reason I did it this way. Hopefully, if it was to be sunny that day, about an hour or so into the drive, the sunrise would give me some extra wind in my sails. That, along with a giant 32 oz. Pepsi.

The night before I did not sleep well. I tossed and turned all night. I think I knew deep down I had bit off more than I could chew. My alarm went off at 5 a.m. Still basically in zombie mode, I crawled out of bed. Marci was still asleep, and I was careful not to disturb her. After gulping down my daily fried egg and sausage with hot sauce, I was quietly out the door at 5:15 a.m.

The roads were deserted at that hour, that kind of post-apocalyptic emptiness you only experience in the wee hours of Christmas day. I had an impossible drive ahead of me, and I was already tired. I thought there is no way I am going to make this trip in one piece, but yet I continued. I was not going to call it off, I couldn't do that. We now had a swimming pool to pay for. Turning around was never even a consideration.

Joliet, Illinois, was supposed to be where the sun rose and brightened my day but it decided not to cooperate. I was forced to continue on in the perma-gray sky I was hoping I'd avoid. With the CD player set to repeat, I watched the entire flat state of Illinois pass by in front of me. In just over six hours, I arrived at my destination.

I pulled into a gas station on the outskirts of town. The seller arrived in a full sized pickup truck. One peek in the back confirmed what I had come for. The whole bed of the truck was packed with plastic tubs of old computer hardware. There was a ton of Commodore 64s, at least twenty of them, along with multiple monitors, disk drives and plenty of games.

I learned early on not to divulge I was a reseller–it tended to rub people the wrong way. Some already knew and didn't care; they just wanted their old junk out of their house. But most people genuinely wanted their things to be used by someone who would appreciate them, and they eventually would, just not by me.

I told the seller I had come from northern Indiana and that I collect these old computers. He gave me an odd look, clearly shocked at the distance I had traveled.

"I wouldn't do it," he said in an arrogant tone.

"Yeah, most people wouldn't," I thought.

But then, I'm not most people.

I neatly loaded up each bin one by one with not a single inch to spare. The seller never said another word and squealed off with his cash.

The drive here alone had taken quite a toll on me; I needed to rest for a minute. I knew what lied ahead, I had to turn around and do the same drive all over again. I shut the rear hatch and walked to the front of the SUV. With a giant thud, I plopped my arms on the hood, took a deep breath and just stood there for a while, scanning the scenery around me.

Off in the distance, I could just make out the Gateway Arch. It was slightly blurry; only the top half of it was visible.

My family had just been to St. Louis that previous fall. Marci and the boys were on break from school, and I had taken some time off from work. We stopped in Springfield, Illinois, and toured Abraham Lincoln's home. We then made our way to the top of the Gateway Arch—well, everyone but me. One peek inside the window-less pods they use to whisk you up to the top was all it took to send me right back outside to wait it out. We had a great time on that vacation, laughing and joking all the way there. I was alone this time around.

A large Red Bull was clearly in order as the poor sleep from the night before made the return drive very difficult. I though about simply pulling over and napping for an hour, but that would have put me home even later. The inevitable crash from the concentrated caffeine only made things worse. I had the cruise control set fairly low at this point and found that resting my head on the seat back was more comfortable. Mile after mile ticked by as I passed through same scenery I had just seen a few hours earlier.

As much as I felt the urgency to get home, I couldn't continue on in this condition. I took a long break at a rest stop. I leaned the seat back and was able to shut my eyes for a while; it didn't help that much but it was something. It was getting later in the day, and I had to get back on the road. I called Marci and asked how everything was going at home. She had gone to the mall that day to buy clothes for the kids. They had acted up in the store as they often did. I could tell from her voice she was stressed from the day.

This run was a different animal altogether. I had finally crossed the line and pushed myself too far. Twelve hours round trip was too much to do in one day. My head was spinning from the long drive. I was wound up and exhausted all at the same time.

My last stop was right back in the place where I was hoping to see the sun that morning–Joliet, Illinois. I lost a quick twenty dollars at a video poker machine and somehow managed to tough out the last hour and a half of the drive.

When I returned home, I found Marci and the boys huddled around the fireplace watching a movie. They were all happy to see me. Even though

I was extremely tired, I did not want my kids to
see that. I jumped right in the middle of them, and
clowned around. I just wanted to see them laugh.
We finished up the movie and I tucked the boys
into bed.

Marci asked me to lie down beside her. I had been
gone all day and she needed some adult time with me.
We talked for a while but I was more fixated on what
I just went through. After an hour, Marci went up to
bed. I told her I would be up soon.

I was still extremely wound up. I had a huge job
ahead of me out in the back of the SUV, and I had
to start on the tasks at hand. Never one to
procrastinate, I was up very late that night testing
the computers.

Finally at 2 a.m., utterly exhausted, my head hit
the pillow.

CHAPTER FIVE

STORAGE WARS

I was pushed by my parents from day one socially and academically. I felt loved by my parents; they provided a good home for me. But whatever I did, it somehow wasn't quite enough. My dad was not the disciplinarian of the family. My mom did not have the support she needed from him and things got rough at times.

After my sophomore year at Western Michigan University, I came back home for the summer. I walked in the door soon after moving back in with the news that I just got a job. I was going to work for the city of St. Joseph, Michigan in their parks department. Basically, I would drive a tractor equipped with a root feeder around town and water the trees owned by the city. I didn't have a contact or friend or any other "ins" to help get me in the door. I just went and got it myself.

The first words out of my dad's mouth were, "How much are you making?"

When I told him I was making just a bit over minimum wage, I could see his face instantly change to disapproval. I felt like all he cared about was what I was earning. My excitement instantly went to a zero. The effort I put into getting it didn't matter. I felt defeated.

I know my parents were both proud of me in many ways; they have both told me numerous times. There was just always a lingering pressure to live up to something else. I would carry that feeling of "never enough" with me into my adult years.

LOT #16 MURRAY, KANSAS

A Craigslist ad had been recently posted for a very large amount of Commodore computers and software. They were asking a very hefty price—more than I had paid for any load thus far. The ad had many pictures that showed all the hardware they had, as well as many boxes full of software. I was able to get just a small glimpse of what was inside but it was all I needed to be all over this lot.

Looking at all the pictures they had posted was very much like the TV show *Storage Wars*, where the bidder is only allowed to look in the storage area, but not allowed to physically walk in there and fiddle around. I knew there was going to be some of those hidden software gems tucked away in those boxes. By this time I knew exactly what each item would sell for and quickly added up my future profits.

I miraculously got the okay from Marci to go. With the distance involved, we agreed it would require an overnight stay.

I called my dad, who owns a black GMC pickup as his utility truck. He uses it for projects in the summer, and snow plowing in the winter. I borrowed it quite often for any projects I had going on. I asked him if I could use it for the trip.

Occasionally the truck would be on the fritz, usually involving some sort of wiring issues. There were times I was advised to, "Keep it running" or I'd be in trouble. My dad said it had been acting up a bit but was pretty confident it could handle the trip. I wasn't too worried. I could wing it. I'd been stranded many times before and like a good Boy Scout, I'd always figure out my way back home. I was all set to make the journey by myself.

The next day my dad called and asked if he could join me. I was a little bit shocked. I was used to going on these runs alone, but I said that would be fine. Marci was relieved I had the extra help and thought it would be good for me to spend some more time with my dad.

I was glad it was just going to be a guys trip. Men don't need a plan. That's a funny difference between us and women. We pack for vacations in the last five minutes and that drives them nuts. If Marci had gone along, she would have demanded a clean bill of health from three different auto shops!

My dad has been a hard worker his whole life. He followed his passion, which was wood working and started his career as a patternmaker apprentice. He later opened his very own pattern shop. My dad believes he truly is the last of a dying breed of craftsmen and still runs his business to this very day.

His pattern shop or "The Shop," as everyone calls it is an impressive building for a one man business. My dad designed and built it himself with the help of his father, brother and friends. It is a large open space filled with lathes, disk sanders and drill presses.

"I'm going back to the shop" were six words I heard almost every night when I was young. There was never enough time from 8 to 5 for him. He had to go back and finish up.

"Times may not always be this good; you have to grasp it while you can," he said at the time.

That made such smart sense to me. These "runs" that I was after were not going to just keep popping up, one after the other each week forever. If business was hot now, I needed to ride the wave.

My dad arrived that Saturday morning. I kissed Marci goodbye, hugged the boys and we were off to get the U-Haul trailer down the street. We soon had everything hooked up and headed out on our adventure. An hour north of Indianapolis was the last time we'd see a major highway. We were taking some back roads through the hilly section of southern Indiana.

The GMC truck had held up perfectly so far; flat steady terrain kept her happy. About four hours into the trip now in the hilly section, the truck started acting up.

My dad immediately leaned his head down to listen a little closer.

"What is it?" I asked.

"Sounds like the transmission."

I heard it too. It was a whining noise, causing the truck to buck a little. My dad tried to smooth out the ride as best he could.

"Are we in trouble?" I asked.

"Not sure," my dad said.

I've been stranded before, but never this far out. We were close to the Kentucky border at this point, and if something was going to happen, our whole schedule would be shot. My dad knew the truck better than anyone. I hoped he was right about it making the trip.

We collectively held our breaths for the next few miles as the truck chugged along, still clearly struggling. The terrain gradually flattened out a bit, and miraculously the noise had gone away. Both of us breathed a huge sigh of relief hoping this was the last we'd hear any strange noises.

A scant ten miles shy of the Tennessee border was Murray, Kansas, our destination. We met the sellers at a storage unit facility. They arrived right at the same time as us. They appeared to be a retired couple. The man and his wife explained that they buy storage lockers and resell them. The man must have done his homework on this particular locker because he had a pretty hefty price on everything. I can usually haggle people down, but this time the seller had the upper hand. He knew the distance I had traveled and was not about to budge.

The seller received his full asking price. We wheeled out each item on carts down the small corridor and into the waiting U-Haul. Pile by pile, we knocked everything out. I did the majority of the heavy lifting; Dad helped with the lighter items.

Our plan was to drive another hour north before stopping for the day. My dad had already looked at our route ahead of time and booked a room at a casino in St. Louis. When we arrived in the parking lot late that night, we needed to figure out where to park. We did not plan ahead and had no padlock on the back of the trailer. After putting our heads together, we decided to park the rear end of the U-Haul as close as possible to a light pole, hopefully blocking any interested parties from opening it. The problem was it didn't block much. Anyone could have helped themselves. After realizing there really was no way to totally secure everything, we just had to let it go for the night. So much for my Boy Scout preparedness.

We arrived home on Sunday at 3 p.m., having made great time on the return trip. I unloaded all the contents into my garage. I could see my dad growing apprehensive about the whole thing. He eyed the loot once it was all stacked up.

"I just don't see how you are going to make any money on this." he said.

Par for the course I thought! Never good enough. Did he think I went all that way on a whim? Why would I attempt something like this if it wasn't a sure thing? I was furious. I just wanted to be complimented. I didn't want to have to justify what I was doing.

I proceeded to walk through the pile and one by one I pointed to each item and threw out the profit I would make.

$100 here.

$50 there.

$150 there.

And so on. I added everything up on the spot. I'd show him this time. I'd go well over minimum stinking wage!

I was tired of fielding the question of whether this whole concept was worth it. Every single run I made was profitable. I didn't want any slack from my dad or my wife or anyone. I just wanted acceptance, and I wasn't getting it. All that made me do was work harder because I thought that is what I had to do.

Murray turned out to be big the biggest score yet. This meant more time moving merchandise and more time in the basement by myself.

Marci mentioned that I was down there working a lot and was not as involved with her as I used to be. Evenings used to be our time to catch up and spend time together. Now, we saw each other at dinner and off I'd go. She got fifteen minutes of quality time with me at best. Marci told me she felt like she had become the heavy hand with the boys.

I agreed to work with her more on kid duties. And I did for a short period of time, but the computers weren't going to sell themselves.

CHAPTER SIX

ROCKY TRAINING MONTAGE

Every lot had a unique story. Some were right down the road, most were hours away. Just when I thought I'd seen it all, something would come along to top the last one.

I give you the Rocky training montage. If you have the song, *"Hearts on Fire"* from *Rocky IV,* now would be a good time to cue it up.

LOT #12 CHICAGO, ILLINOIS

An ad for 500 floppy disks appeared in suburban Chicago. Like a hobo on a hot dog, I was all over it. The seller asked that I come to his house instead of meeting somewhere because he needed to be home to "watch" his mother. I figured she was in bad health. Come to find out, nope, healthy as a horse. He was clearly pushing 40 and still rocking his geek's paradise down in mommy's basement.

LOT #58 ROCHESTER HILLS, MICHIGAN

I secured the deal over the phone. The plan was I would pick up the computers that were to be placed on the front porch. After my three hour trip, I arrived with no boxes in sight!

I supposed I was due for a scam at some point. I called the seller, who claimed she forgot to put them out, and she and was currently on her way to the Upper Peninsula of Michigan.

That was it; I guessed I was burned. After a brief moment she came back on the phone and said to just use the garage key code and go in the basement and get my stuff.

"Ooookkay," I thought.

Beep-boop-boop-beep.

I was in. Straight down the stairs I went and I'll be darned–there were the computers, boxed up as promised. A very weird feeling came over me. I was in someone's house I didn't know; the neighbors did not know me. Was this going to end well? I placed all four boxes in the back of my SUV and closed the garage back up.

"That was too easy," I thought.

Feeling a little crafty, just before leaving, I gazed up and noticed a security camera pointing right at me. She'd been watching me the whole time! Realizing this, I smiled, tipped my invisible hat and went on my way.

LOT #15 HEBRON, INDIANA

One weeknight run found me woofing down my dinner and rushing out the door to Hebron, Indiana, an hour away. There was a dude who actually beat me by a few minutes on an ad that was giving away a ton of computer hardware. He picked them up and turned right around and reposted the same haul later that day. I knew I still could make a nice profit and went to get it. On my way out I congratulated him for having the fastest fingers.

VEGAS BABY!

I received a voicemail out of the blue one day. A woman explained to me she sources items to be featured on the TV show *Pawn Stars*. The show depicts a real pawn shop in Las Vegas and is about all the interesting "treasures" people bring in. Customers get their items appraised, and usually the seller is shocked by the value of their item.

She asked if I would be okay with them using one of my computers for the show. I'm not one who craves the spotlight, but the wheels started turning, and I figured I could get a free trip to Las Vegas out of this. I asked how that would work if it was technically my item. The woman explained either I could be on the show as myself or someone would he hired to "play" me. You know, for that extra reality TV authenticity.

"How about you use me on the show and you can use my item?" I offered.

She obviously needed someone to fit the look, so I was asked to record a video of myself using the product much like I would if I was selected for the show.

After a couple of practice takes with Marci, it was time to roll film. I played the part the best I could, demonstrating how the "rare" computer worked. In the end, my mug did not fit the look, and my TV dreams were sadly squelched.

LOT #55 CLEVELAND, OHIO

Shortly after a nice score in Ohio, I found myself down in the basement going through the haul. I was quietly testing things out when suddenly I was hit with most noxious smell I have ever experienced. I wasn't sure where it was coming from at first. I turned to the pool table workbench and spotted an old power supply belching yellow smoke and making an awful sizzling sound. Those old power supplies were known as the "brick" because in the middle of the cord was a heavy square section that housed a large transformer. I feared I only had seconds until the thing exploded and pulled the plug as fast as I could. I quickly whisked it outside to be hosed off holding the smoldering demon by the tail like the poltergeist-trapping machine from *Ghostbusters*.

LOT #19 TAMPA, FLORIDA

You can't keep a good picker down! Spring break with the family in Tampa found me stealing our convertible Mustang rental car for a computer run. My boxes were piled so high that the convertible top had to stay down for the return trip. The family became my little elves that night, as they wheeled everything up to our sixth floor condo in shopping carts.

I had just acquired a whole carload of vintage computers 1,200 miles away from my house. Not a problem: four boxes full of hardware were easily mailed home, three computers were sold on ebay while still in Florida, and the remaining items were strategically divvied up amongst the family's luggage. Games were slipped into my laptop bag, computer keyboards were stuffed into the nooks of our large suitcases, joysticks and power supplies filled out the kids' carry-ons.

"My backpack is heavy!" they both cried.

"Hey, you want a swimming pool don't ya? March!" Sergeant Dad had spoken.

CHAPTER SEVEN

PRE OCCUPATION

I am a graphic designer by day. I love what I do. I always knew I wanted a career where I could be creative. In previous jobs I was a cook instead of a waiter. Now I am a designer instead of a salesman. It suits where I like to be, behind the scenes, but still the creative pulse.

Always willing to take on more, I started my own graphic design business in 2013. After a couple of slow years, I picked up a good amount of business. Now, my computer picking gig had become job #3.

I think somehow I was predisposed to fall into this type of thing. About 15 years ago I thought it would be fun to buy a metal detector, so I did. I ended up using it quite a bit. I had my own special technique.

When I heard the beep indicating something metal was present, I took out my trusty screwdriver and proceeded to repetitively stab it into the ground. Then I listened carefully. Metal objects would make a different sound than the soft soil and when I heard that sound, it was time to pry up the find.

I kept a jar full of all the treasures I have ever discovered. Coins are the most popular item but I have also dug up keys and rings. On a well-worn path in a ravine behind my grandparents' house, I unearthed my oldest find—two mercury head dimes. Those were minted from 1916 until 1945 and very rare. Metal detecting was so fun for me because you never know what you are going to find. Computer picking was now providing that same thrill and along with it very good side money.

On a typical morning I would get up and work on the tasks at hand. Usually overnight some ebay sales would take place and I would need to box the items up, get them labeled and out to UPS that same day. Fortunately, UPS was right on the way to work. I got to know almost everyone there. I was usually greeted by Ann, Katie, or the owner, Mark. Mark would always give me a hard time if I was a bit off schedule.

I'd hear, "You're late!" If I walked in at 8:30 a.m. With a chuckle I would agree and promise to see him the next morning.

Lunch breaks were spent either driving back home as quickly as possible to list some more auctions or getting some fresh sales ready to go out the next day. Evenings were also prime time to get work done. I spent many late nights down there in my hole on the pool table work bench.

Each and every item I listed needed to be cleaned, tested and photographed before it was ready to go on ebay. Many computers had years of accumulated crud on them, smoke smell, even random gifts inside. One lot came complete with a different member of a stink bug family inside every unit. It was like the toy surprise you'd get in your cereal box.

If you were sloppy and claimed something worked when it didn't or were not clear on your description, it could result in returns and possibly negative feedback from the buyer. I learned to be extra careful about details like that, I wasn't about to tarnish my 100% positive feedback rating.

My ebay auctions were always hopping. In fact, I had nonstop active auctions to attend to for a three-year time span. I liked to have something to track all my finds, so I made a map of all my adventures and labeled each city I have ever visited. After my St. Louis disaster, I updated the map with a big circle indicating the maximum comfortable driving distance for a day trip. That key distance was about four hours one way in any direction. The map was actually very handy giving me an instant read of what was accomplishable in a day.

I started to spend some of the profits. A huge TV for the basement blew the boys' minds one Christmas morning. The in-ground swimming pool went in that following summer. Things were happening all over the place and I was extremely busy at this point. With all the craziness going on, I still found a way to make all three jobs work and not neglect any one of them. The one thing I was starting to neglect was my family.

One particular night while things were hectic at home, my sons Bowen and Tad were a little rambunctious. Bath duties were in order as well as homework. I yelled for them to get the tasks at hand completed. I was working in the basement on a disk drive, and they were upstairs. The unheeded requests quickly turned into threats to take away their electronics.

"All you care about is your stupid Commodores!" Bowen shouted.

I shrugged it off as simply an upset child who didn't want to do his chores. I should have dropped what I was doing and attended to him right then and there, but I didn't.

CHAPTER EIGHT

THE MOTHER LODE

A sunny Saturday morning in October found the family volunteering for the first time with our new church. Marci signed everyone up to do some work at a local campground. We needed some quality family time. It was easy stuff–cleaning tables and spraying weeds. We were all enjoying our day together.

A couple hours into the task, *Ding!* goes the e-mail alert on my phone.

Game on.

LOT #41 GRAND RAPIDS, MICHIGAN

I had no idea what I was in for based on the Craigslist ad. All it read was, "Multiple vintage computers." It had no pictures at all. The seller gave me an address of where to meet him. When I arrived

at the destination, I saw that it was a storage
locker facility.

Not able to get inside, I called him. He said he
would meet me at the main office, and then we'd
proceed into the lockers area. A few minutes later,
the man pulled up and signaled me to follow him in.
We stopped in front of a large storage locker.
He opened it up.

This was not a few boxes in some guy's garage.
This lot was unlike anything I had ever found so far.
The locker was basically the entire contents of one
man's whole life. The seller must have bid and won it
due to non payment by the renter. I didn't ask how
it all went down. I was too awestruck at what lied in
front of me.

There were dozens of Commodore Amiga
computers stacked halfway up to the ceiling. These
were not Commodore 64s; these were the next
computer they produced in the late 1980s, and these
were much more sought after and valuable.
Everything imaginable Amiga was there. Software by
the box-full, monitors, books, disk drives–you name it,
this guy had it. I was not about to leave without it.

I put on my best poker face and threw out a
good offer.

The seller countered.

"Okay I can meet you halfway" I replied. "That is all I have on me."

With a handshake, the seller left with me the storage unit key code and the garage door padlock key. I quickly filled my SUV as full as possible. I had hardly made a dent in all the items I needed to move.

I immediately called Marci, my hands still shaking with excitement.

"Well, how did you do?" she asked expecting the usual run of the mill story.

"Where do you want to go?" I said.

"What??" she replied.

"You are not going to believe this. We can go to Europe with this haul!"

We had a few recent conversations about my time commitment in all this. It was starting to wear on her and the rest of family. This would change things, I thought. The sheer magnitude would simply blow her away this time. I'd show her it was all worth it.

I just made my dinner plans with my extended family in Kalamazoo, Michigan, that evening, still in disbelief over what had just happened. I scheduled a U-Haul pick up for the very next morning. I thought it would be fun for my oldest son Bowen to come with me.

Bowen has a mind like no other in the way that he is able to notice the smallest detail and retain it. There have been many instances where I simply can't figure out a technical problem. He'll look at it for a second and say, "Here, you just use this."

He has a tendency to walk a couple of steps behind the rest of the family. It often irks Marci and me, who are always racing toward the next thing. Bowen is simply moving at his own pace, taking the world in. Sometimes I wish I could slow down and see the world through his eyes. I think it would be good for me.

He accompanied me in the passenger seat of the U-Haul to Grand Rapids. The cabin so big with so much to see; he felt like second in command that day. When we arrived, I unlocked the door and started in on the rest of the pile, carrying everything into the trailer piece by piece. Bowen grabbed a couple light things but got more excited over headphones and chargers he found still new in the box. I let him have the pick of the unit.

We took a break for lunch and ate right there at the locker. I kept thinking that this just couldn't be

63

real, what I just scored still hadn't sunk in. I still had a long ways to go. After four hours, the last of the contents were stuffed into the U-Haul. A few scragglers were left behind. But that wasn't my problem, I was out of there.

At the end of the day the entire contents of that storage locker had now filled half my garage. One wall contained computer books from floor to ceiling. Another wall consisted of a huge pile of floppy disks filled with software. Along the back wall was the hardware stacked on top of each other. In the center of the garage was a mountain of boxed computer games. It looked like I had purchased the entire contents of a computer store that was going out of business.

I took a moment to stand back and take it all in. I just stood there processing everything, trying to come up with a plan. It had all finally become real to me. I decided this was simply too much to piece out and posted my own Craigslist ad, something I had never done before. I had always resold on ebay. The ad read, "The Amiga Mother Lode" and I had a huge asking price.

The online Amiga community soon caught a whiff of what had transpired and were collectively wetting their pants from the news. It spread like wildfire. My e-mail in box exploded. Fellow computer nerds–er, aficionados–contacted me and asked if I was a collector and why I was unloading all of this. Others offered to help identify hardware for me.

I had one very knowledgeable fan who was extremely helpful. If I took a picture of a computer part I did not recognize, usually some kind of expansion board, he was able to instantly identify it and e-mail me right back. He was not even buying my stuff. The guy just wanted to help out.

I even had some visitors. One fan from Chicago actually made three separate trips to my house. He did some "shopping" in my garage and took home some Amigas and some games. A wild-haired man from South Bend, Indiana, also visited and was brought to his knees by the sheer sight of it all.

"Oh my God, this is like my biggest Christmas wish come true!" he cried.

I had a few bites on my ad but ultimately decided to piece it all out. I could make a lot more money if I did it that way. This was going to require months of hard work. This was the only time I felt truly overwhelmed at what lay ahead of me.

One technique I found that I like to do is find a rare item and set up my ebay listing as a "no reserve" auction. That simply meant I had no minimum price I had set beforehand. I just let it ride. The highest bidder wins. If you have the right item, you get a bidding war going.

About halfway through my mountain of goodies in the bottom of one of the boxes, I found an old three-ring binder with a Commodore 64 logo on it. It was slightly worn and didn't look like much to me. I initially tossed it. A day later before the trash went out, I had second thoughts. I took another peek at that old folder and thought, why the heck not? I started an auction with no reserve. Turns out, I had something rare indeed! The bidding was furious. In the end there were over 25 bids, all for an old folder I almost threw away.

As I watched the profits add up, I grew even cockier. Nobody can pull off what I am doing, I thought. Nobody has the guts to travel as far as I do. I even combed ebay to make sure there were no competitors near me doing the same thing. I didn't want anyone else grabbing my stuff. Not that there was anything I could have done about it if there were. What was I going to do anyway, go take them out?

Thanksgiving quickly came and went, then Christmas. Finally, at the end of January, it was finished. A whole storage locker was completely pieced out and resold. I don't know that I even saw the sun that whole time. This was by far the craziest thing I had ever done in my life.

I was ready to reap some rewards. Marci and I discussed taking a family vacation to Europe at some point. We also talked about going on a mission trip. In the end, I treated myself to a luxury sedan. I blasted *Hair Nation* from my new car like I was 18 again, letting the whole block know I was coming.

Marci received spontaneous gifts as well. I'd run into Macy's after nabbing a nice load and pick up presents for her. I thought I would be happier with all my new toys. But I wasn't.

CHAPTER NINE

I GET EDUCATED

I got to know the Commodore line up very intimately during my reselling gig. Being an extremely popular computer at the time, it spawned many different models. An all-in-one portable variant with a tiny screen known as the Commodore SX-64. A business-only model dubbed the Commodore Plus/4, which failed miserably. And even a model with double the ram—a whopping 128K called, you guessed it, the Commodore 128. I thought I knew everything about the Commodore brand but I soon found out there was still much to learn.

LOT #67 INDIANAPOLIS, INDIANA

A very interesting ad popped up on the e-mail. The ad was for a Commodore Educator 64 computer.

Surprisingly, I had actually never heard of this model. The computer looked almost identical to the fairly common Commodore PET, a personal computer dating back to the late 1970s. I figured this was a sister model and worth about the same.

I made contact with the seller and found out he was going to be free later that week. We set up a meeting place north of town. I headed out on a nice late summer morning.

U.S. 31 connects South Bend and Indianapolis. It's an old thoroughfare seemingly cursed to be eternally under construction. One of the biggest improvements was the Kokomo Corridor Project completed in 2013. It knocked a half an hour off the commute and eliminated about thirteen traffic lights. You could also really haul some serious ass on this stretch, which I often did.

The meeting place we agreed on was Lowe's in Carmel, Indiana. Arriving with ten minutes to spare, I took a quick bathroom break. As I walked through the store, I couldn't help but notice every single person was dressed in their after church Sunday best. At first I though maybe my calendar was off by a couple days, but then realized, nope, it was just a typical Friday morning. Man, I love Carmel!

I waited outside at the garden entrance of the store. The seller arrived right on time in a pickup truck with a covered bed area. He explained he had done some work for an old lady who happened to have this computer in her garage. She said he could take it off her hands for $50. He was a very happy camper to sell it to me for four times that.

Little did I know I was about to be "educated" on just what I had here. Wikipedia.org provided some background information, as well as a couple of short videos on YouTube. I learned that the Commodore Educator 64 was briefly used in school classrooms and was supposed to be a worthy competitor to the Apple II computer. That never happened, and it quickly faded into obscurity.

A quick check of ebay found exactly zero models actively listed or recently sold. I had nothing for comparison to work with, I needed more information. If this was indeed just a sister model to the Commodore PET like I thought, I would surely have found something by now. Hoping to dig a little deeper in ebay's archives, I went back to Google and typed in my revised search parameters:

"Commodore 64 Educator 64 ebay"

Bingo!

I found a completed auction for the exact model I just purchased. It had sold for twenty five times what I bought it for! Instantly giddy with excitement, I ran to tell Marci about my find. I did a little dork dance right there on the spot, and kissed the computer like leprechaun that just found a pot of gold. She thought I was nuts.

When you have something that rare and not seen on ebay in many years, you price it accordingly. So I did just that, I went big. After a few weeks right before the listing was about to expire, I got an offer. I ended up selling it to a buyer in California.

I had a few mishaps over the years with monitors that I thought were well packaged only to receive an e-mail informing me they were damaged in transit. I was not going to take that chance this time around, not with this item. I dropped the computer off at UPS and used its packaging service. They packed it all up and assumed all responsibility in the event of any damage.

Three days later, I received an e-mail from the seller. I was in the car at the time. I glanced down and saw the email subject pop up on my phone. I immediately screeched to the side of the road fearing the worst. When I opened the e-mail I was relieved to see it was only the seller informing me everything was okay. My baby had arrived safe and sound.

Without missing a beat, another run popped up on the following Saturday. It was such a good score, I needed to get it as soon as possible. I knew there would be other interested parties. My son Tad had a soccer game scheduled for that day. I explained to Marci this was too good to pass up. There was no other option—I had to miss his game.

On my way home I got a call from Marci, who was not happy about the back to back runs I was making.

"Well I just made a nice buck ..." I crowed thinking that is what she wanted to hear, but was quickly interrupted.

"I don't care if you make million dollars. I want you home!" she demanded.

I was flabbergasted. Did she not appreciate the money I was bringing home? On what planet was this setup negative in any way? Did she not comprehend the sheer amount of work I was putting in for my family? We fought quite a bit on the phone. I hung up fuming.

I did not want to slow down at all and carried a lot of anger with me over that conversation. I never stopped to look at it from her perspective. That was why I didn't tell her about my next plan right at first.

The next one I had cooked up was so over the top, so positively ludicrous, I knew it would be met with strong objection.

My next run had been in place for a few days. I needed to let Marci know what I was working on, but I dragged my feet. When I finally did tell her about it, I got the usual bevy of questions and concerns. I fielded all the questions, but I was tired of answering them. This went on for a couple days.

On the third day, Marci brought up one final concern. I knew these were going to be the last words we'd speak on the subject, as my stubborn self had a track record. I wasn't going to change.

"You know this is crazy," she said.

"I know," I replied.

CHAPTER TEN

THE LONG AND WINDING ROAD

What do you do when you are going to Los Angeles for business but have an extra day to play? For most people it would probably be go to the beach. For me? Start searching for treasures. The LA area proved to be dead, so I had to expand my search. Just like clockwork, an ad popped up. Only it wasn't in California.

LOT #69 PAYSON, ARIZONA

The ad already had me at "Fourteen boxes of computers and accessories," despite the fact that it had no pictures. This was a very big gamble. No pictures? Who the heck has no pictures? I asked the seller that very question. He explained the camera on his phone was broken. Plausible, but something didn't smell right about this. Either I was going big or going for bust.

I was staying in Los Angeles for six days for work. I had a graphic design conference at the convention center scheduled for that week. After landing in LAX, I walked to the rental car location. Expecting a misaligned Hyundai as my mid-size generic selection, I was floored as my brand new Mercedes C300's open doors greeted me. Just 15 miles on the odometer! Sweet.

I didn't factor in getting out of Los Angeles county to my drive time, which I was estimating at seven hours. I knew it would be longer with traffic, but that number was easier to stomach in my mind for some reason. I had dealt with LA traffic once before. You know you've got a serious infrastructure problem when you hop on the freeway on a Sunday morning at 8:30 a.m. and traffic is already at a standstill.

Once past Palm Springs, I finally made some headway. This is also where the terrain became extremely boring. The highway signs indicated Desert Cities were up ahead. One by one they came and went followed by long stretches of basically nothing. Five hours into my trip I hit the Arizona border. Holy crap, more desert.

I soldiered on to much the same scenery until the big city of Phoenix, which by that time was too dark to see much of anything. Halfway through the city, I turned and headed due north for my final hour of the drive.

A casino was the last known sign of life for the next 65 mind numbing miles. I was very tired at this point, and this stretch was proving to be quite challenging. I had to slow way down on a number of occasions because driving at this point became more like a video game. It didn't seem real. No road goes on this long with nothing, I mean nothing, to break it up. And the curves? It was all curves, not a straightaway to be had.

I started to worry about what I was going to find. A wave of fear came over me. Something said this was all going to be a huge disaster, something was off about the whole thing. I could have been having a great time in California right now just relaxing. It was dark, I was fatigued, and my mind was conjuring up crazy scenarios.

I made a right turn and was on a side street that looked like there were some actual signs of human existence once again. The street had quite a few houses. It winded around and turned into a decent-sized subdivision. After eight long hours on the road I had just two lefts and there would be my destination. Finally.

I parked in the street in front of the seller's residence and made my way past three unfinished project cars hogging most of the driveway. The area was poorly lit, no street lights were on and just a single interrogation-style light bulb lit the man's entire garage. I traversed the maze of junk on the floor and made my way to the back door. On the ground next to the door were the boxes, all 14 of them, just like he said.

The seller came out the door. He looked like an extra that just walked off the set of *Wayne's World*. He was a very talkative guy; I found out he was out of work at the moment, and the money he received was going to go towards fixing one of his cars. We chatted a bit and I gave him the cash and loaded up the car, one box at a time. He helped me with each one, following me out to the car with a different story about his life every time.

He asked if I was going to stay in the area for the night. I told him I was going to go up the road a bit and find a motel. He was more than happy to help me find a place, not with his phone but with a relic from the past, the Yellow Pages. Old school like me, I liked this guy!

His wife had come out of the house at this point and helped out as well, informing me there was a Knights Inn just past the Burger King in the next town up the street. It was in the wrong direction, but I didn't care. I was not about to drive through those curves again, at least not until tomorrow's daylight.

The pristine new Mercedes was now filled to the headliner with boxes of disk drives, joysticks, power cords and some local critters having surely taken up residence inside the contents years ago. I looked like *Sanford and Son* had traded their truck for a European sports sedan.

I was pretty much an expert on packing a car full of computer equipment at this point. I learned early on how to best fit the contents. Small heavy pieces started on the floor in various cracks and crevices and served best as dead weight. The next layer were the boxes. They created a sturdy mid-level platform for any further loose items that were piled on top and continued up to the ceiling. Once again, I had not an extra inch was to spare as I drove off to the next city in search of a hotel.

Yet another casino earmarked the border of the next town, Payson. The town had a clean, touristy feel to it. It was pretty deserted at this point. I selected the Knights Inn as my final stop.

Being way too keyed up to settle down, it was time to take a peek at the haul. I grabbed three boxes and carried them into the hotel room. Indeed this fellow had some treasures! I uncovered many rare games along with expansion cards, and giant strands of power cords. I weeded out a few duds and sent them to the motel's one trash bin.

Soon I felt I had a grasp at what I had and even created enough room in the car for me to see out the back window. Still, I had to know what else I had in the car, so I made two more trips for more boxes. Then I discovered something I had never come across, a boxed game called "*Zak McKracken and the Alien Mindbenders*." It was made by Lucasfilm Games in the late 1980s. Yes, that Lucasfilm.

I had only seen a couple of these on ebay. This was big. Not the holy grail of collecting but a very rare gem indeed. This one game alone already had me into profit territory. I propped the box up against the wall to proudly display my find. This little guy is going to ride shotgun on the way home, I thought—and he did.

Morning came and out the door I went. I felt refreshed to simply have some sunlight and to be able to see everything I missed the night before. The drive faired somewhat better as I snapped picture after picture out of the window. A call home caught my family just leaving church. I was able to talk with the everyone.

My youngest boy is Tad. A little clone of myself. Sometimes I think the similarities are uncanny. He is a glass is half empty kind of a guy, a realist. He calls it like he sees it. A funny thing he does when he watches movies is call them out for running over the alloted critical time frame. It's usually something along the lines of diffusing a bomb with just two minutes left the countdown clock. He'll keep time in his head and is ever so quick to declare, "Hey, its been way over two minutes!"

Tad wants word definitions, trivia, factoids, super long words. He soaks it up like a sponge. I think he acts so grown up for his age, but then something so small and innocent reminds me that he is still just 10. He's still learning his way and still needing a strong influence in his life. We talked about the desert scenery and how I was so excited to see my first cactus. Before we hung up, Tad told me he missed me.

Once back in LA, I was yet again in the sticky situation of having another huge pile of computers and being very far from home. I was with my design team from work. I didn't want to use up my time alone selling computers. I had anticipated making this score ahead of time and had already packed my tape gun. It came in very handy as I quickly packaged up four boxes of hardware and sent them home to Indiana.

I also had to get creative with my suitcase situation. I stuffed five loose computers and a couple disk drives in my large suitcase. It felt like it had a small person inside. I though what the heck, I'll probably just get charged just a little more at the airport.

Turns out my suitcase weighed in at 80 pounds and the extra charge was $75. The woman at the airline check in counter informed me I needed to be under 50 pounds. She was very patient about it and let me go down to the end of the line and reshuffle some things around. I finally managed to swap enough items into my carry-on and get the big suitcase under the critical 50 pound limit.

The TSA people of course flagged my items as they went though the scanner. One employee even recognized a Commodore 64 and asked me about it. I had to endure the typical swabbing and extra layer of security. I knew that was coming though. In total, all the extra nonsense added about an hour to my check-in time.

After landing in South Bend, Indiana, I made my way to the baggage claim area. A few minutes later, I spotted my tattered suitcase, power cords shamelessly exposing themselves to the rest of the world as they hung out the unzipped edges. I was finally back home, my treasures in tow. I had pulled it off once again like I always did.

By the way, final mileage count 27 hours later on that sweet Benz–978 miles.

CHAPTER ELEVEN

THE RIGHT PATH

When I got home from California after six days away, the whole family was thrilled to see me. We all hugged for a long time. Bowen and Tad were especially happy to see me. I saw such excitement in their eyes, something I had not seen or maybe simply not noticed in such a long time.

I saw right at that moment in their eyes, their love for me. All this time, I had been on cruise control. I was physically there but yet I wasn't. My heart softened. Suddenly, everything came into perspective.

My life had become nothing more than a never-ending cycle of searching for the next lot and claiming the bigger prize at the end. My life had become that stupid game I played when I was 12.

I just kept repeating the same task over and over. There was no end. No matter what I achieved it was not bringing happiness. I told myself I was doing the right thing by making money for my family, but I was really losing them in the process.

My boys are curious about the world and come to me, their dad. I had not been fully attending to their needs. I was not putting them first. What kind of a father has his head buried in a stupid disk drive and can't even drop what he is doing to answer an innocent question? A pathetic man like myself consumed by his own interests. I did not want to continue on like that.

Marci and I love the pastor at our new church. Pastor Tony is a younger guy, just a year older than myself. During his sermons, he'll often start off with a funny story. Then he gets into the meat of the message. He knows just when to break it up with an audience participation event. Marci always comments on his preaching style. Being a teacher herself for 23 years, she can appreciate what it takes to engage an audience week in and week out.

I really felt like I could connect with Pastor Tony because he is close to my age and has been through a lot of the same experiences I have.

One of his sermons was about the subject of what we do with our gifts and abilities. Our pastor posed the question: Do we keep them and serve only ourselves? Or do we use the gifts we have been given for the glory of God by making disciples of all his people? Marci and I were both so moved by that sermon, we went up to Pastor Tony that very next Sunday and told him it was exactly what we needed to hear.

Pastor Tony hadn't given his life to Jesus until his late teen years. He was a bad kid as he described himself, selfish, with no direction in his life. He said the closest he ever felt to God was when he was dead broke, hopeless and simply cried out and prayed. I wanted more of a connection with God for myself. I wanted to be happier. The more money I made, I felt like the less I relied on God. It was like money was my security blanket; it would take care of me.

I changed my nightly prayers. For forty-some years they had been the canned variety:

"Now I lay me down to sleep, I pray the Lord my soul to keep. If I die before I wake, I pray the Lord my soul to take."

I then blessed everyone in my family, deceased pets included. I thanked God for everything I had and prayed for him to watch over me. Only a handful of times, when I had some serious issues going on, I would deviate from the script.

It was not personal. It was meaningless. Earthly possessions are not really ours, everything we have belongs to God. I now asked what I could do to just simply be happy right now. I prayed for the right direction in my life.

It was now late November 2018. Christmas was quickly approaching. I had found yet another small run and told Marci about it. She sat down next to me on the couch. She didn't express any questions or concerns. Marci just asked that after this run I take a long break through the holidays. Up until now, I always maintained that I had to get these, I had never even once considered stopping or slowing down. This time my response was different.

"Okay, I will." And I meant it.

It was time.

CHAPTER TWELVE

THE LAST RUN

I don't think I realized it at the time, but I had carried that feeling of pressure with me my entire life. The day before I left on my last run, Marci uttered the words I will never forget.

"You don't have to do this anymore."

She accepted me for who I was and didn't demand any more. Those were the exact words I needed to hear all along. I felt like a huge weight had been lifted off my shoulders. I would still go on the run, but this time it was different.

LOT #71 KALAMAZOO, MICHIGAN

I found an estate sale this time around as my run. I could hit the Michigan border in ten minutes and reach Kalamazoo in exactly an hour. I had one last vacation day to burn up at work, so I took that Thursday off.

I immediately thought of inviting my dad. He would be coming from St. Joseph, Michigan, and could be there in less time than it would take me. I asked him if he wanted to meet me there. He agreed. After a couple of phone calls to direct him in, we arrived at the sale about 20 minutes early.

The property was roped off, and the estate sale people were busy setting up. My dad was very interested in how these sales work. I explained that when you arrived you got a number with your name on it and then when it started, they called you in order to enter. The earlier you got there the better. I had heard about people arriving the night before to camp out for these sales.

The house was a vintage picker's dream. It was chock full of electronic goodies. The owner had old Macintosh computers, an Odyssey2 video game system and tons of Atari cartridges. There was also a good amount of my brand there as well.

I scoped out the section of the house where my Commodore 64 hardware resided. I was going to head there first.

The clock struck 8:30 and we all entered in

numerical order; we were #25 and #26. I instantly headed over to the house, leaving my dad to grab items in the garage area. Seconds later, I had four armloads of disk drives. Fortunately, there was a woman with the estate sale company sitting next to me in a doorway to help me start some piles. I was able to get almost everything I had set out to get.

When I came out of the house to walk to the checkout area, my dad came rushing up to me. He had found an old Apple III software box.

"Hey, do you need this?" he asked.

"Yes, that's it! Thanks for finding that!" I said.

We both smiled, proud of our teamwork. He did great in his helper role and didn't question what he thought I could clear this time. I paid for everything just as the snow was beginning to fall.

We decided to head just down the street to McDonald's. Senior coffee for Pops and a large dollar Coca-Cola for me. I felt very relaxed that morning. Even with the snow now catching up to me that I had outrun in Indiana, I was in a good mood.

We spotted another picker from the estate sale there. He was there alone. I asked him how he made out. The man explained he was after old tobacco pipes.

My dad and I talked about his upcoming kitchen makeover. He said he needed to stop at the store. He had helped me with countless projects over the years, so I was more than happy to go with him for one of his projects for a change. We stopped at Menards to look at counter tops and drawer pulls before heading our separate ways. The whole morning turned out to be some nice father-son time.

I don't resent my father. All I ever wanted was just acceptance from him. He made some mistakes, but everybody does. I definitely have. There were so many positive lessons he taught me. I still remember these three instructions he gave me when I was young and about to start my first job.

"Be on time."

"Go over and above."

"Ask what other tasks can you take on."

Those were well spoken words of advice from a man who achieved great success but always stayed humble in the face of everything that was given to him.

I drove straight home through the now heavy falling snow. I had just finished lot #71. Since December of 2015, I had picked up, processed and resold over one thousand vintage computer-related items.

My estate sale finds were resold just like everything else, but I wasn't in the usual rush. I tended to them periodically, when time allowed for it. I knew I would never top what I had already done, and no longer felt the need to. I looked forward to the holiday break with my family.

CHAPTER THIRTEEN

RECONNECTING

I often went to Sunday brunch after church growing up. The occasion always included my grandparents and sometimes my uncle and cousins. It was always at a nice local restaurant. We'd usually shy away from the chains. I'd always get the buffet and usually over-stuff myself. I would declare I was done eating for the day, but by the time dinner rolled around I still found a way to include that last meal.

One day I thought, you know what? I want those same kinds of memories for my kids.

On the Sunday right before Veterans Day, I asked Marci if she wanted to go out for lunch after church. It was quite out of character for me. There were some Sundays I would actually sneak out of church early to make a run. Marci was floored by my request.

We didn't need to rush home; it was Sunday after all, it should be a day of rest. We all enjoyed a relaxing meal and reconnected. I learned more about what my kids had done that previous week at school, stories I would have never heard had we just headed straight home.

I took an extra day off from work before Marci's and my adults only weekend trip to Louisville, just to tool around town together. We tried out a new place for lunch, then saw a matinée. We took a note out of Bowen's playbook that day and just slowed it down and took our time. I felt like a had a whole new outlook on things.

What I really enjoy is trying new activities with Marci. That is how you develop a deeper love for your partner. Just doing something out of the ordinary, together.

"Something has changed in you," she said.

"What do you mean?" I asked.

"Well for starters, you asked me to go out after church. That isn't like you. In the past, if I would have mentioned going out for lunch you'd have said, *Are you crazy? We have perfectly good lunch meat in the refrigerator!*"

It meant so much to Marci just to spend time together on a weekday, time I would have normally used to get extra work done. I had forgotten that the little things make such a difference to her. I had been neglecting her needs and putting mine first for too long.

My life so far had been very goal oriented. I had now achieved everything I wanted to. Instead of just being able to see a huge mountain of challenges and milestones ahead of me, I felt was now over and on the other side of the proverbial "hill." I needed to have all my experiences that I had to finally put things in order. Only then could I gain wisdom and see what was truly important.

While I proudly boasted I had those three jobs, I was neglecting my most important job, which was being a father and a husband. What I failed to realize all this time was one simple thing.

My time with my family is more valuable than any amount of money I could ever make.

One night I asked Bowen if he wanted to play pool with me. I taught him how to hold the pool cue with his fingers spread out for support. I told him to make sure you line up your shots and always follow through. He was really interested in playing with me.

After the game, I expected him to rush back to his phone like he often did. But this time was different. He kept talking about the game, asking about trick shots and hitting a few more balls for practice. I enjoyed teaching him.

Tad and I took in a movie over the holiday break. I knew there had to be a good old '80s flick he would like. *War Games* proved to be right up his alley. There was something very gripping for him about this movie. During the scene where Matthew Broderick's character was on the news for hacking a government computer, I glanced over at Tad. The normally tough critic who could smell a bad film a mile away was mesmerized; hanging onto every frame. It brought back memories of my experience when I first saw it in 1983. I reacted the exact same way.

My last auction ended on the week before Christmas 2018. It was just some old joysticks and cords. I boxed it all up just like every other item I had ever sold and took it to the UPS store the next morning.

"Just the one?" Katie asked.

"Yeah, just the one" I replied. "Have a Merry Christmas."

That was it.

There was nothing else to sell.

Christmas morning came. Most of the presents were wrapped ahead of time and already placed under the tree. The big morning reveal like years past was no more. The boys were older now. Inside Bowen's largest gift was a brand new pool cue. We went downstairs that morning. The antique pool table, covered and used as a workbench for the last three years, was still cleared off.

We played a game. I noticed his skills had improved. His grip was better and he followed through on his shots. He had listened to my instructions. I let him win, just like my dad did for me.

THE END.

Telengard

1912 Brunswick
pool table

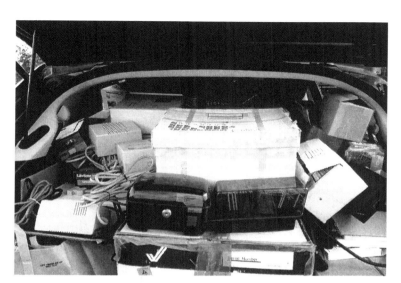

A typical score

The Commodore
Educator 64

Payson, AZ

The schoolhouse in La Grange, IN

107

The mother lode

Pat & Bill Husek, Bowen and Tad Husek

Marci, Bowen, Brian and Tad Husek

Keeping hydrated
while editing

111

Made in the USA
Lexington, KY
16 January 2019